Marcy Schaaf
Joe the
Bee Rescuer

Welcome to the buzzing world of Joe the Bee Rescuer! In this delightful story, you'll meet Joe, a brave and kind-hearted hero with a special gift for talking to bees. Using nothing but a cardboard box drizzled with honey and his cheerful spirit, Joe helps his neighbors find gentle solutions to their bee problems. Join Joe on his whimsical adventures, and discover how even the smallest acts of kindness can make a big difference. So, get ready to buzz along with Joe and his bee friends in this sweet and playful tale!

Joe had a super power: he could talk to bees!

Whenever a bee problem buzzed, Joe came to the rescue.

Joe wore no special gear just cap and a big brave smile.

With a cardboard box and honey, Joe worked his magic.

One day, Mrs. B called,
"Help! Bees in my garden!"

Joe arrived, waving, "Hello, little bees, follow me!"

He drizzled honey in the box, making it extra sweet.

"Come on, bees! This way!"
Joe gently coaxed them.

The bees buzzed happily, following the honey trail.

One by one, they wiggled
into the box.

Joe smiled, "Good job, bees! Almost there!"

Soon, the box was buzzing with happy bees.

Mrs. B smiled, "You did it, Joe! Thank you!"

Joe grinned, "Happy to help! Bees are my friends."

Next Mr. Courser called
"Bees in my attic!"

Joe grabbed his box and honey, ready for action.

"Hello, bees! Let's find a new home," Joe said.

The bees buzzed excitedly, following the honey scent.

Joe guided them into the box,
gently and carefully.

"Great job, bees! You're safe now," Joe cheered.

Mr. Courser thanked Joe,
"You're amazing! Thanks"

Joe chuckled, "It's all in a day's work!"

Joe loved his bee-saving adventures.

Bees were his buddies, and he loved helping them.

From gardens to attics, Joe was the bees' hero.

With his honey box, he brought joy everywhere.

Joe taught everyone, "Bees are friends, not pests."

And the bees? They buzzed happily ever after.

Thanks to Joe, the BEE-MAN, brave and kind.

And that's the sweet end of our bee story!

Good Night!

Books By Schaaf

www.BookBySchaaf.com

Find us at: